ON BLUE ICE:
The Inuvik Adventure

Author, Co-ordinating Editor:
Jane Stoneman-McNichol

Outcrop
The Northern Publishers
Yellowknife, Northwest Territories

Town of Inuvik
Inuvik, Northwest Territories

ISBN 0-919315-05-4 (hardcover)
ISBN 0-919315-06-2 (softcover)

ACKNOWLEDGEMENTS:

This book is dedicated to the people who built Inuvik and to those residents of yesterday and today who left their mark upon its history.

It is dedicated also to those who gave so freely of their time in relating oral histories and donating photographs and in offering invaluable assistance in compiling this work.

Contributing Writers:
Bernadette Hardaker
Ilse Hirschegger
Greg Smith

CO-PUBLISHERS

Outcrop Ltd.
The Northern Publishers
Box 1350
Yellowknife, N.W.T., Canada
X1A 2N9

Town of Inuvik
Box 1160
Inuvik, N.W.T., Canada
X0E 0T0

Printed and bound in Canada.

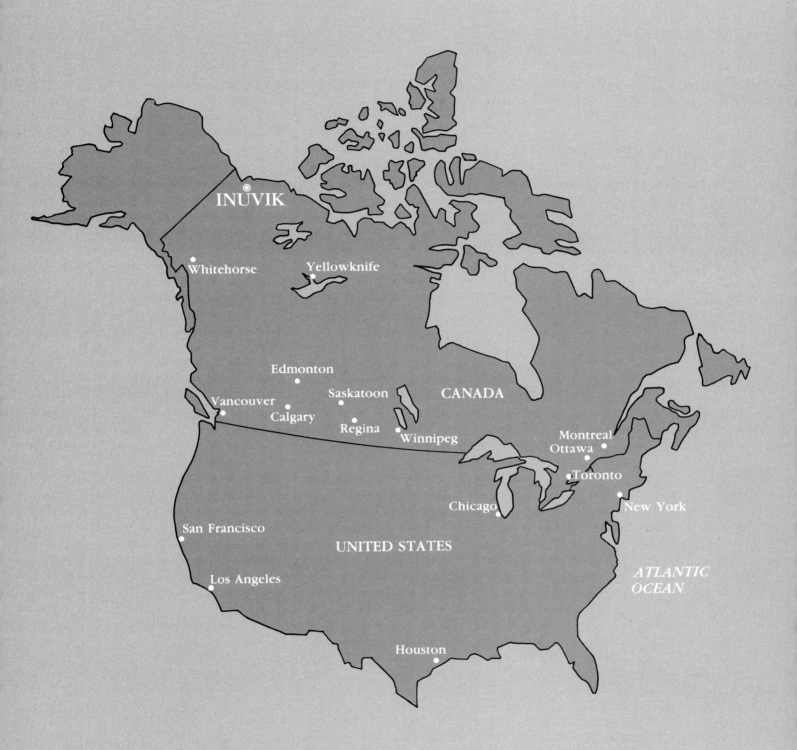

INUVIK

Whitehorse

Yellowknife

CANADA

Edmonton

Saskatoon

Vancouver

Calgary

Regina

Winnipeg

Montreal
Ottawa

Toronto

Chicago

New York

San Francisco

UNITED STATES

Los Angeles

*ATLANTIC
OCEAN*

Houston

Footprints break the winter landscape near Boot Lake.

TOWN OF CONTRASTS
'An Arctic Oasis'

Inuvik was unique from the outset.

Never has a community in Canada been so thoroughly planned, researched and documented. It is a town conceived by the mandarins of Ottawa and built by hands that had previously skinned muskrats and set snares in the Delta.

"Inuvik" is the Eskimo word for "Place of Man". Located 1920 air km north of Edmonton, 100 km south of the Beaufort Sea, the Town of Inuvik lies on the east bank of the great Mackenzie River. On cold mornings the sun peeps over the horizon sending pink rays ahead. The ice fog retreats across the winter landscape as the long shadows move from west to east during the few lighted hours each winter day. At dawn the stillness that blankets this northern town is broken only by the perpetual hum of the massive generators at the power plant. The town is a contrast to the silent endless landscape.

The concept of Inuvik was born in Ottawa in 1954.

Early that year, the stamp of approval was placed on the planned development of Northern Canada's first "model" town. A few short months later a helicopter carrying site-planning engineers hovered over an area where previously only wildlife had witnessed the predawn exhibition of colours. Geologists and surveyors began the arduous task of site-selection. Several requirements had to be met.

The Mackenzie Delta muskeg does not have good soil conditions but a stable area had been located adjacent to the Delta on the east side of the East Channel of the Mackenzie River. This channel separates the Delta from the rolling tundra to the east. Here were abundant gravel deposits, room for an airport, fresh water lakes nearby and a navigable river chain. This site met all the requirements for a new townsite.

As sub surface and surface surveys progressed, equipment and materials were barged down the Mackenzie River. Manpower was recruited in southern Canada and surrounding settlements in the Northwest Territories.

The construction itself was a series of innovative feats. The men adapted southern technology to overcome the adversities of building in the weather conditions of the Arctic.

One of the greatest sociological experiments of our history began as the townsite neared completion. Residents of the neighbouring settlement of Aklavik and the Delta moved to their new home.

Simultaneously, southern Canadian technologists and administrators were relocated with their families to the new town. A period of mutual adaptation began. Native northerners and those who chose to make the North their home have always been adaptable and this contributed to the development of a community social fabric in the pioneering 1950s and into the oil and gas boom in the late 1960s and early 1970s. It continues today.

There were many native northerners without formal education adapting to southern technology. They were accepting a more structured lifestyle far from the traditional seasonal life they had known. At the same time southern Canadians were learning to adapt to life in the Arctic.

Today the town itself is a study in contrasts – contrasts as stark as the bright winter sun on a blanket of new fallen snow.

Inuvik is a place where the sun sets the first week of December and appears again in early January. It is a place where a crowd will gather on a Saturday night for a traditional drum dance at Ingamo Hall while others stay home to toy with their home computer centres.

Inuvik is a place where native people leave their town homes for bush camps in the spring as New York City crews descend to film commercials.

The town is characterized by high rollers whose thriving businesses are waged and sometimes lost in poker games.

It is a place where residents gather at the riverbank as the first resounding crack of ice heralds a short spring and a long awaited summer.

Inuvik is a cosmopolitan centre that in less than 30 years has undergone social and technological change which in another epoch would have taken a hundred years.

In 1953 only the snowshoe prints of an occasional trapper broke the snow-covered ground where the airport runway lies today. In 1982 Pacific Western Airlines moved 18,000 passengers out of Inuvik over that same stretch of land.

Asked to describe his home one old-timer replied:

"You can't describe Inuvik. You have to experience it."

Perhaps, after all, he is right.

Tents on the riverbank to house the construction crews in the early days at East Three

BIRTH OF A TOWN
'Building on the Blue Ice'

Inuvik's story began in the years just after World War II, when Canada's government decided it should establish a permanent communication centre in the Mackenzie Delta. The centre would serve the Western Arctic as an education, transportation and administration hub.

The natural focus for development and establishment plans seemed at first to be the existing community of Aklavik. Aklavik had been for many years the trapping and trading capital of the Delta. It became an important transportation terminus and since 1920 when the Royal Canadian Corps of Signals set up CHAK, the first settlement in the Territories to have a commercial radio station.

Aklavik, at 68° North on the Peel Channel of the Mackenzie River Delta had a wealth of history on its side. It had been the traditional meeting-place of Inuit and Dene hunters: its sloughs and snyes produced muskrat pelts of quality high enough to attract eager traders, including the Hudson's Bay Company, which established a trading post there in 1912.

Aklavik's many virtues at first impressed government planners but they were faced with a number of difficulties. The most questionable factor was the mud.

Aklavik was built below flood level on the unstable silt of the river delta. When the Mackenzie River ice broke up in the spring the settlement was frequently flooded. Buildings shifted on their wooden sills as the waters of the mighty river system surged past. When the floods receded, they left behind a soggy quagmire which often sucked a pair of rubber boots from the feet of their surprised owner. The residents laughingly referred to their home as the "Mudtropolis of the North." The engineers were not amused.

The end of the muddy summer season brought with it more hazards: the freezing ground heaved and buckled, damaging the buildings that clung tenaciously to the Delta's slippery surface. The planners shook their heads.

There was one further problem, perhaps the most insurmountable of all to the engineers, architects and bureaucrats who wanted to build a growing new town of the future out of Aklavik.

There was simply no place to grow.

Aklavik was hemmed on all sides by lakes, swamps, and marshland. There was no room for the expansion that was the heart of a vision of a northern "model" town.

The Advisory Committee on Northern Development decided that Aklavik would not do. A new site must be found and a whole new community built – from the bottom up. Every detail would be precisely planned and orchestrated, from the time the first construction post was sunk, to the laying of the last rooftile – nothing would be allowed to go wrong.

First the site must be located. The perfect site for the perfectly planned community of the not-yet-named town of Inuvik.

In 1954 Ottawa's Department of Northern Affairs and National Resources dispatched a survey team to the Delta.

The surveyors carried a precise set of criteria. The new location must score high in all the following ways: the area must be large enough to fit long range expansion plans. It must have soil with a high gravel content as a source for construction fill. It was preferable that the townsite be located near a navigable channel of the Mackenzie to serve as a shipping jump-off to the Beaufort Sea; there must be a fresh water supply and an expandable airport site; and, obviously, the new site must be above flood level.

For months a small Bell G47 helicopter piloted by Don Landells carried survey teams to the northern sites. The Delta was gridded and criss-crossed countless times. Data was coordinated to narrow the field of selection; then the few best possibilities were minutely examined all over again.

Finally, the choice was made. On the site designated "East Three" by the engineers, at a spot on the East Channel of the Mackenzie River 100 km south of the Beaufort Sea, Canada would build its model northern town.

"Before there was any Inuvik here – there was nothing. Quite a few people trapped through this town. There was Pascal, the old trapper, Baptiste, Joe Adams and Albert Ross. This was just traplines through here."

—*Catherine Mitchell*

The countryside surrounding the new townsite had seen little change since 1789 when Alexander Mackenzie paddled by on his voyage to the Sea. Grizzly bears still roamed the Richardson Mountains to the west. The barren-ground Caribou migrated to the southeast. Hunters and trappers still trekked by snowshoe over the virgin snow. Wildlife was everywhere.

The new townsite met the planners' specifications and yet it was not perfect. There were many technical difficulties to be overcome in the construction.

Permafrost would be the greatest problem.

Arctic construction is complicated by the "blue ice" that lies always beneath the surface of the soil. As the name implies, permafrost never completely melts, and below the new townsite it reached downward 1,000 feet. In winter the freezing extends down from the surface; in summer the top few feet melt away under the intense rays of the 24 hour arctic sun.

Sometimes this process is complicated by removal of three or four foot layers of insulating tundra. This happened at Aklavik when engineers trying to build an airstrip gouged away the topsoil, leaving the permafrost to melt down very deep – and turn into a quagmire that melted down eight to 10 feet in the first summer.

Visit of official party to East Three, August, 1954

No one wanted to repeat such blunders at the new townsite.

Engineers knew that heat from houses would melt the permafrost just as easily as the sun's rays had done. They decided to set their buildings on wooden pilings driven deep into the permafrost. This would create breezeways beneath the structures and the ventilation would disperse the concentrated air and not contribute to the melting of the permafrost.

Once the planning reached this stage, it was time for the project to roll.

Only about 60 days a year are frostfree in the Inuvik area. While the warm weather of 1954 lasted, crews began a frenzied stock-piling of lumber on the river banks. Equipment and materials were barged in and covered to protect them from the ravages of winter storage.

The following summer construction would begin.

Among the people of the Delta, there was disquiet about the new development. The trappers had seen the surveying and the planning on their traditional hunting and trapping grounds and they watched this activity with interest and a measure of apprehension. They were being urged by the government to move to the new site.

"I came over here just after they brought in the lumber the first summer. They left it piled on the riverbank for the winter. During the winter it burned down. They always suspected the local trappers of burning it because they didn't want a town built on their traplines."

—Freddie Carmichael

The following summer more supplies, more equipment and more workers were needed. The opportunity to draw a regular wage for their work opened for many people of the North for the first time. They no longer needed to rely on the erratic, unpredictable income from hunting, trapping or fishing.

"When I first came here I got a job cutting the brush at the beach. We lived in tents. We didn't get paid much – about $1 an hour. That was a lot then. You could buy cigarettes for 75¢ a package in those days."

—Tommy Ross

Far up the Mackenzie, trees were cut to provide wood for the piles or "stilts" on which the buildings of the town would rest. The wood was piled on the

Unloading construction materials at townsite, Fall 1954 "Radium Charles" (tug)

riverbanks and a barge from Hay River was loaded with its cargo and chugged towards the new site as the waters flowed after spring breakup.

Meanwhile down the river at Aklavik the first barge of building material was loaded together with two prefabricated warehouses. The warehouses would store the insulation, nails, tools and hardware for the new site until more supplies arrived from the south.

The barge, pushed by the Yellowknife Transportation tug the "Sandy Jane" left Aklavik for the new site and was expected to arrive in about 10 hours. The workers watched the channel and waited – and waited.

"We were waiting for that first barge to arrive from Aklavik and it was overdue. Later we learned that the tug had taken the wrong channel and gotten hopelessly lost. They turned south at Gallagher Arey's camp and became confused. The tug made a new channel through a chain of shallow lakes. They came upon a flabbergasted biologist, Eain MacEwen, who showed them on the map where they were. The tug pushed south to Pascals Channel and onto the East Channel.

Here we were in town watching for the tug to come from the north and it chugs up from the south! I think the captain was quite embarrassed over that one!"

— *Mike Zubko*

Out on the Delta there was growing excitement. Caught up in the curiosity about employment and improved living conditions some made a first attempt to visit the site.

"We could see the town from our bush camp out across the lake. We were tired of eating fish and ducks and 'rats'. I sent John Dillon and my youngest daughter Beverly over to the camp to see if they could rustle up some oranges or eggs – anything different.

They came back with nothing and Beverly was upset. They had crawled up the bank and peeked over and saw a big sign that said NO WOMEN ALLOWED. She was afraid they would shoot her or something so they ran back to the boat and came home."

— *Agnes Semmler*

Agnes and Slim Semmler ran a bush store and a mink ranch out in the Delta. Undaunted by the sign, they moved with their growing family to the new site. There were many families who followed.

"The first time I came to Inuvik they were cutting willows on the riverbank. There was only one tent. I think it was Dan McLeod who was the cook and I remember going into the cook tent and having a cup of coffee. There was absolutely nothing – just a barge coming up the river with supplies. There was nothing here but the tent."

— *Marie McInnis*

There may have been nothing at the beginning of that summer but the engineers and their crews set right to work to change that.

The site hummed with activity.

Day and night a helicopter swept up the river carrying engineers; barges chugged the river bringing lumber and supplies; trucks and tractors were unloaded from the barges and lumbered over the unbroken tundra; bulldozers plowed ceaselessly into the gravel pits; cranes hoisted wood piles, and steam drills blasted post holes into the permafrost for foundations. Everything and everyone was moving.

The Department of Northern Affairs stressed a vocational training program for Delta residents. The contractors at the site were urged to place trainees on the payroll. One of the earliest vocational trainers was "Dusty" Miller. He and his wife, Connie, arrived in Inuvik to a pioneering project. Connie Miller would become one of Inuvik's first school teachers.

Dan, Rosa and Ellen McLeod beside cooktent

Camp for airport construction crew

Construction crews, under the supervision of instructors like "Dusty" Miller, blasted test pits throughout the surrounding site area. They were trying to determine the depth of the gravel they would need for construction fill. Tommy Ross, an Inuit raised by a Loucheux family, worked on one of those crews. Today he has his blasting papers from his on-the-job training.

"I remember we made 107 test pits here in Inuvik. The deepest pit I recall was 105 feet of gravel. We went down that deep and then we hit clear blue ice!"

—*Tommy Ross*

The East Three site had been a prime choice because of the abundance of birch trees. Those trees indicated that good gravel conditions existed below the ground cover. C. L. "Curt" Merrill was Project Manager of the teams of engineers at the new site. He was respected by the workers. He was also adamant about the delicacy of the Arctic environment.

"Everyone knew they had to be very careful around the trees. Curt Merrill would have shot anyone who cut down one of those birch trees!"

—*Barney MacNeil*

Curt Merrill also had the unenviable task of selecting sites for both the Anglican and the Catholic Churches. That selection was fraught with more difficulty than the engineers had encountered with the new townsite. His instructions were simple. There was only one requirement – that each location be better than the other!

Notwithstanding the humour of some of the situations encountered, everyone working on this unique project realized the significance of this new site's undertaking. Every step of the way problems were overcome by new methods of research, planning and construction.

In the construction phase, top priority was given to the airport. It had to be located convenient to the townsite and equipped to give year-round service. The site chosen had a rock base which would be blasted and used as fill.

The location was approximately 12 km from the townsite in a well wooded area. A special design was drawn before the construction began. There was no room for errors which might cause later heaving of the airstrip. Trees were cut and laid on the ground and this layer was then covered with limestone fill

Steam pile driver smashing wood piles into the permafrost for the foundation of a warehouse, Inuvik, 1956

from the blasted rocks. Even today the airfield remains in excellent condition.

The construction of the airfield was undertaken by Aklavik Constructors Ltd. under the foremanship of Henning Jensen. The airport was built at the same time the townsite was taking shape. There were two distinct construction camps as a result and a primitive road linked the airport site to town. People still joke that it was easier to fly the workers into town than it was to drive the road.

"There was a road all right. It was really just a bulldozed path."

—*Agnes Semmler*

"I remember the first day I went over that road. It was just rocks and dust and heat. Karla was sick she was so scared. Oh, it was terrible."

—*Dawn Zubko*

The construction crews continued to work around the clock during the short summer period. The townsite contractors were Montreal Engineering Ltd. and Poole Construction Ltd. By the summer of 1956

the townsite was taking shape. The 24-hour sunlight during the short Arctic summers can play tricks on even the most seasoned residents. The foremen were no exception.

"Our foreman was Adolf Kozicek. He used to trap up the Anderson River. He would be up at seven in the morning hollering his head off for us to get working. Sometimes he would lay down after supper and wake up and it would be seven o'clock. He thought it was morning so he would yell at us to get to work. He only did that a few times!"

—*Tommy Ross*

The next job to tackle was construction of the road surfaces. Building roads over the Arctic soil became another of the many challenges. Everyone recognized that few forms of road construction would be more difficult or expensive than building on permafrost. Permafrost is relatively impermeable to moisture, so drainage was a problem. Ditches were out of the question because they would destroy the insulating moss cover.

Because of the permafrost the engineers had an insulating layer of moisture-free gravel laid several feet thick on top of the ground surface without disturbing the moss and overburdening the surface cover. This insulating cover would prevent the permafrost from melting.

To overcome the drainage problems in construction, the engineers designed the roads to follow, as closely as possible, the natural contours of the land. Drainage would be by run-off.

As road construction proceeded some of the design decisions were questioned.

"Originally I came from Montreal where the streets are narrow. When I moved to the West of Canada I was so happy to see big, wide streets and avenues. The first time I walked down a street in Inuvik after they were built I thought to myself 'Well, it had to be Montreal Engineering the streets here are narrow too!'"

—Barney MacNeil

"I thought it was very strange that we had such narrow streets here. I thought they could spread things out more and give everyone more room. One day I said to Curt Merrill, 'You have a million square miles in the Territories. Why did you let them build the streets so narrow?'

He looked around and laughed and said to me, 'Don't worry Nels, we'll have angled parking!'"

—Nels Hvatum

Some of the first buildings were the "512's". These were houses so named because they were 512 square feet, a size designated to fit an exact number of four by eight plywood sheets. As housing was completed people were moved out of the tents by the river that had been home for many months.

"We had lived in the tents down by the river in the winter time too. It was a 12 × 14 tent with a wood frame and we had an oil stove."

—Tommy Ross

Houses were being erected on the east end of the town site and the network of the utilidor system was built to coincide with the completion of the apartments. Branches of the utilidor system were later built to service the Hospital and the nurses residence.

The "utilidor" system was an innovative answer to the question of how to build a water and sewage system which would remain relatively untouched by the subzero arctic winter temperatures. Today the aluminum box-like insulated structure snakes throughout the town linking houses with sewage, water and heating services – the sun glinting from its metal exterior.

Like the housing and building structures the utilidor system is raised above ground on wooden pilings and gives the appearance of a long freight train of box cars frozen in stillness.

"We all marvelled at what an innovative system the utilidor really was. They ran a cold water pipe through it and then a hot water pipe to keep the other pipes warm during the winter. They used the hot water pipe as a source of heat too for the town. Then there are the flow pipes for the sewage in and out. Watching them build it was quite an experience!"

—Ken Snider

Building the utilidor

Sawmill at the river's edge, circa. 1955

Core drilling on townsite, 1955 - sampling permafrost

Day after day the steam-driven pile driver pushed the wooden piles deep into the permafrost. The sound of hammers striking nails echoed throughout the site. Housing was being erected. The airfield was well under way and road construction was progressing.

The government continued to encourage people of Aklavik to move to the new townsite. Generous compensation was offered to property owners of Aklavik and lots were provided at the new town free of charge to anyone who wanted to move. The government warned that the usual government services at Aklavik would soon be discontinued and concentrated at Inuvik. They reiterated their warning that planners had determined that homes in Aklavik might disappear into the shifting soil. The townspeople of Aklavik did not take that statement seriously.

"When the government decided to move Aklavik they asked the people to move over to Inuvik. Those people had already settled there. They had their home there. There was this big idea that Aklavik was going to disappear one of these days – like an island – just be gone, sinking. It's just like anybody from down south. If they have a house there they don't want to spend the rest of their lives here. They want to go back. Those people didn't really want to move."

—Edward Lennie

For some the idea of moving was adventurous.

"We were living in Aklavik at the time that a move to the new site was announced. We were quite excited about moving over to a new townsite. The original concept was to abandon Aklavik and move the site to the west – closer to the mountains. But that was a miserable site. The mountains created stronger winds. It would have been hard to land a plane and the mosquitos over there were terrible. I was quite pleased when they considered the east side."

—Mike Zubko

The people from Aklavik remember the severe winds that marked the winter months. They talk of tying ropes between the buildings and holding onto them to find their way in a storm. The biting, swirling winds of an Arctic blizzard made visibility almost nil. It was easy to lose your bearings. Newcomers were always warned not to go out alone in a storm.

Close-up of steam hammer driving piles at town wharf

"When the storms started you could actually see them coming down the river just like a wall. But not over here. I've never seen a storm that bad in Inuvik."

—Dawn Zubko

The new townsite, though only about 50 km from Aklavik and further from the mountains, offered a more sheltered environment from those harsh Arctic winds. During the summer months the marshes surrounding Aklavik had attracted swarms of mosquitos. It was hoped that the new site, atop a plateau and further from the marshes of the lake, would alleviate the "bug" problem.

Any new townsite needs stores to provide services to the growing population and this site was no exception. When Agnes and Slim Semmler moved over to the new townsite from their bush camp they opened a store in a tent on the river bank. The year was 1955. the store had no floor.

"Instead of sweeping dust from the floor like most people would – we shovelled out the mud!"

—Agnes Semmler

New Hudson's Bay Post, Inuvik, August, 1957

There was a camaraderie amongst the new towns-people. They socialized with each other, organized dances and even fought over the few women in town as dance partners.

There were different construction crews employed at the site and they felt an intense rivalry with the "airport gang" who occupied a construction camp 12 km out of town during the building of the airfield. The rivalry existed over the lack of women. The men in town felt they had first "dibs" on the women.

In 1958 another recreation centre opened where the rival "gangs" could meet and enjoy a dance, a game of pool or a cup of coffee. It was the "Rec Hall" owned by Stan Peffer and managed by Cece McCauley. Today the building houses the Dene and Metis Office and Rita's One Stop Shop.

The construction camps competed with the Rec Hall for staff. The larger camps could offer better wages and room and board. It was a difficult position for the enterprising private individuals to compete with but they rose to the challenge.

"When we were building the Rec Hall it was so hard to get help. Sometimes you had to go out in the morning and drag some of the men in to help. I even lost my own sister to one of the government camps. I couldn't blame her though – they were paying more than $3.00 a day with room and board. I couldn't compete with that."

—*Cece McCauley*

Communications with the outside world were certainly less than ideal in the early days. The military had their own communication links and others shared what was available. There was no telephone in the days when construction was being completed. Communication relied on the mail delivery by airplane.

"Before the airport was built here the larger planes like the DC-3 would land at Norman Wells and then the smaller planes with skis would come down the river. That was once a month, then twice a month and then weekly.

When the airport was developed you could fly in here all the time. It really made a difference to the whole area."

—*Mike Zubko*

"Those were the days if you were flying out to a settlement you asked if anyone had mail for you to take. Once scheduled air service came in later on you didn't do that anymore. But you wouldn't have been too popular in the early days if you arrived without mail."

—*Freddie Carmichael*

It was an exciting time. The new town site already had its first baby born in a tent on the riverbank where "Happy Valley" campsite lies today.

"I was born October 24, 1956. They said I was born in a tent down by the river. They said I had lots of nurses and people around and they were all fighting over what to name me and they came up with 'Shirley'. There were no doctors then. Just nurses and midwives. My mother said it was really cold out the day I was born."

—*Shirley Allen Kisoun*

Background:

Curt Merrill, Project Manager (L)
Charlie Walrath, Resident Engineer (R)

Foreground:

John Gilbey, Dept. of Agriculture,
Ft. Simpson (L), Frank G. Cunningham,
D.N.A. & N.R., Ottawa (R) 1955, at
Inuvik

THE GOLDEN DAYS OF RADIO

"Hello Chee Bee Chee — used to be CHAK!"

With these infamous words the "Trapper" calls in to CBC Inuvik to share his unique view of the world from a bush camp in the Mackenzie Delta.

CHAK are the old call letters of CBC Inuvik back in the days when radio was a seven person operation.

The roots of CHAK go back to the settlement of Aklavik when Red McLeod of the Army Signals Corps built a transmitter from scrap. The 25 watt station was run by volunteers and a dime would buy you a chance to send a request to your favourite gal or guy.

Nellie Cournoyea, now MLA for the Western Arctic, got her start in radio in Aklavik and eventually became manager of CBC Inuvik.

Wally Firth, the first native member of Parliament, was the first voice on air from Inuvik on November 25, 1960.

Today, CBC Inuvik employs 30 people. It broadcasts in four languages (English, Hareskin, Loucheux and Inuvialuktun) and is heard from Fort Franklin to Sachs Harbour and from Old Crow to Cambridge Bay.

Weather conditions were unusually good during the construction seasons and the townsite was soon in place. By the fall of 1958 the Northern Canada Power Commission would have completed installation of a 150 kilowatt diesel generating unit to supply later construction requirements, with the additional capacity of two 375 kilowatt units for use as the population increased in the coming years.

The Hudson's Bay Company opened its first store in 1956 coming only a year after the opening of Agnes and Slim Semmler's store. The first church was the Catholic mission opened by Father Brown in a tiny house he built himself. Later on the beautiful landmark "Igloo Church" would undergo construction. For the meantime, Father Brown even started a small newspaper which he printed himself to keep everyone informed of the town happenings.

Construction of the future hospital, school and residences, government garages and warehouses, airport, fire hall and Canadian Forces Base was well underway.

As the townsite framework grew, so did the sense of community spirit. With that spirit came the desire for a town name. Residents didn't enjoy being referred to merely as the "East Three" residents. Those who had moved from Aklavik felt that confusion would result if the new site was named "New Aklavik". They had fond memories of their previous home and wanted its name to remain unique.

The push for a name was on.

After much discussion throughout the area, Knut Lang of Aklavik, the Mackenzie Delta elected member, proposed to the Council of the Northwest Territories a name choice for the new site.

The Council of the Northwest Territories met in Ottawa from July 14 - 18, 1958 to consider proposals on various northern matters – the naming of the site was one.

On July 18, 1958 then Commissioner of the Northwest Territories, R. G. Robertson, declared by Proclamation that the settlement "sometime known as Aklavik East Three be known as INUVIK".

INUVIK, the Eskimo word for "Place of Man" – a townsite with a name of its own – a future to look forward to.

New Federal building and RCMP headquarters under construction, Inuvik, circa. 1956

New hospital, Inuvik, 1961

GROWING PAINS
'Urbanizing the Arctic'

When Inuvik's engineers set to work, there was no precedent for a planned, ambitiously large-scale town in the Canadian Arctic. The physical problems of creating the urban unit were immense. But once the town was built, social issues of even greater complexity had to be tackled.

One of the reasons for Inuvik's creation was the need to provide education for the Delta's children, to whom schooling had previously been unavailable. The logistics of this were complicated by the fact that most of these lived in small and widely scattered settlements.

The solution at the time was to bring the children to the school, and the hostel idea became a reality.

During the summer of 1959 the finishing touches were put to the newly erected school and hostel facilities. In early autumn the first planeload of children from the scattered Delta settlements arrived. They would live in one of the two hostels throughout the school year, and would not go home again until the following June.

Two hostels were built, Grollier Hall for Catholic children and Stringer Hall for Protestants. The hostel residences were managed for the Department of Northern Affairs by the Roman Catholic and Anglican missions.

Town children and hostel children went to school together, though even in the classrooms they were separated.

"I remember all the Catholic children were in one wing and all the Protestant children were in the other. The Catholics had nuns for teachers. They were always separate from us – even on the playground."

—Karla Zubko

The hostels offered jobs to many townspeople. They were needed as supervisors for the kitchen and dining room, and recreation activities after school. Residence supervisor's for both boys' and girls' wings were hired.

"When I worked as a supervisor at one of the hostels I couldn't leave at night until the children went to sleep in the dormitory. One night one of them kept sitting up in bed and I kept yelling for him to go to sleep. It was dark and I couldn't see who it was. Finally, I went down with the belt in my hand and here it was Mr. Holman, the residence manager. One of the little boys was sick and he

brought him something from the kitchen. He was so good to the children. He thought it was funny that I was there with the belt."

—Catherine Mitchell

Classroom separation became impractical as numbers dwindled on one side and mushroomed on the other. To alleviate overcrowded conditions, students were transferred with parental permission from the crowded wing of the school; religious distinctions were therefore minimized, and the barriers dropped. All children, regardless of religious background, were educated together in the same classrooms.

In spite of these difficulties, the children settled into their new environment with relative ease. Many of the townspeople did not. There were deep-seated social concerns.

The development of Inuvik and its surrounding areas has been disruptive of the traditional way of life in the Delta. It is argued that the native people were expected to make too great a change by moving to Inuvik and leaving the home they had always known.

"It was hard for the natives to get used to things here at first. They had a tradition as nomads. Their hunting grounds were seasonal and they moved with the seasons. They just weren't used to staying in one place all year round."

—Nels Hvatum

Outdoors class in early summer, Inuvik, 1960

Children arrive from settlements to attend school, 1959

First houses on Distributor Street at East Three

Newly erected government row houses at Inuvik, 1961

Some of the residents, however, feel that it may not have been as bad as later sociologists liked to believe.

"These people are very adaptable. When the first kickers (outboard motors) came out the Indians and Eskimos caught right on. It was better than paddling a canoe. There were advantages and disadvantages but these people will readily accept change if they see an advantage. The change did affect us all."

—Mike Zubko

Notwithstanding the natives' ability to overcome drastic change in their way of life, there was a certain tension over the government's housing policies. The tension resulted not only from the lack of developed housing for the native peoples but also from the expectations of government personnel from the south.

"We thought all the people would be mixed together just like in Aklavik. One white lady from the south came here thinking that her children would have Eskimo and Indian playmates. She was here for several months before she even got to the other end of town to find that that was where they all lived. You see, the government built houses at one end of town and put their people in them. If you were a native working for the government you didn't get a house, you lived in a tent."

—Dawn Zubko

For people from Aklavik who were reluctant to leave their homes to move to the new townsite, there were enticing offers of housing. The offers themselves created confusion.

"The government told me if I moved they would give me a little lot. They said that the rent I was paying would help buy my house later. They gave me a receipt for it and I paid out more than $3000. One day I realized that I paid more than I should have and Daisy Harrison told me that was because I was paying for the land too. If I was as smart then as I am today I would have gone around and asked some people what was going on, but I never said nothing. I just paid."

—Catherine Mitchell

The government had supplied housing for the personnel who would arrive from the south to assist in the administration of the new townsite. They had also provided permanent housing for native or southern people who wished to purchase the "512's" in the west end of town.

There was still a need for housing for those tenacious individuals who occupied tents in Happy Valley and were not entitled to government housing. Agnes and Slim Semmler were in private business, and were among the many families who later constructed their own dwellings.

Children dwarfed by their new federal school, Inuvik, 1960

In spite of all these problems, the new townsite with its up-to-date services enabled the population to enjoy a higher standard of living than they had ever known in the bush.

"It was getting into October that one year and everything was freezing. You'd get up frozen and have to light a fire to warm up the tent. My son Buck and Evan MacLeod came in from the DEW Line and built a little shack for us.

"We moved in before it was finished and they just worked around me. Later on, I had one little electric light. It was the first time in my whole life that I had electricity. They put one little wire to the house from NCPC. I felt like I was a queen."

—Agnes Semmler

As the housing situation improved, Inuvik's residents overcame their differences. They recognized that the very newness of the town had created problems which they must learn to solve together.

"There was a feeling in the community that it was really coming together even though the services to the town were only in the east end. There was quite obviously a push by the government and the residents of the west end to see that they too in fact had the opportunity to hook into this wondrous thing called the utilidor which would haul water and other services. The people realized this was better than having to lug your own water and sewage back and forth."

—Jim Robertson

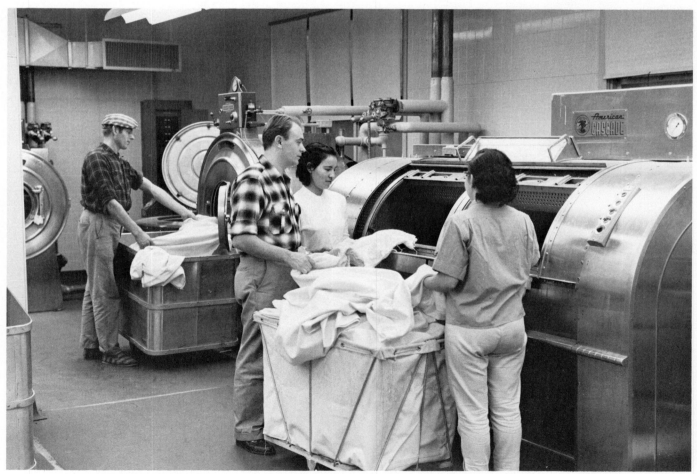

John Komaromi, manager of the new Inuvik Laundry instructs in the use of the circular washers

The construction period was virtually complete. The need for trained personnel, skilled in research technology and administration, was growing. Before long, a major influx from southern Canada began. Many of those early southern emigrants still live in Inuvik today.

"I came up here to be the first Director of the Scientific Research Laboratory. I had technical training in scientific research, and that was one thing they needed here."

—Dick Hill

For most of the native people as well as those from southern Canada, employment meant working for the government or with one of the contract companies maintaining town services.

Businesses were springing up.

The Canadian Imperial Bank of Commerce opened a branch, and became not only Inuvik's first bank, but Canada's most Northerly bank of the time. The Mackenzie Hotel opened its doors. The Hudson's Bay Company established its store, in competition with L. F. Semmler's General Store. Pacific Western Airlines moved their office in.

Private entrepreneurs were also setting up shop. John Komaromi opened the Inuvik Laundry and became an employer of many people who had previously worked only in the bush. His business thrives today.

"When he opened the laundry I went to work there. It was the first job in my life where I got a paycheck."

—Agnes Semmler

The new town of Inuvik was a source of opportunity for the enterprising. The residents have always been characterized by their ability to start from scratch. They were creative with new business ideas, even though their backgrounds in such matters had often been limited. In fact, lessons of survival learned on the land were often usefully applied in the new setting. Skills acquired in Aklavik helped, as many businesses opened and flourished. Most of these survive today and many have expanded. The smallest idea could grow into a viable commercial venture.

Men were not the only entrepreneurs in the new town. A number of women initiated and ran new enterprises on their own or with the help of other women.

"I started the Inuvik Craft Shop with nothing but an empty store. It was really from scratch. I ordered things from Coppermine, Aklavik, Tuk, and Holman Island. I always ordered on credit and sold things on consignment. As I sold things I paid off the bill. That was the only way. There wasn't any money to do anything else."

—Agnes Semmler

Today the Inuvik Craft Shop has changed hands and name. It is now "Northern Images", and is well-known across Canada as a shop where carvings, paintings and handmade parkas are available.

Inuvik was a town where success meant hard work, long hours and most times, doing the job yourself – even if you were the Manager.

"I managed the Rec Hall then. It was only women who ran it in those days. We didn't have any men in here. We ran this place in the beginning with no running water, no sewer, no toilets. Can you imagine? I emptied my share of those darn honeybuckets!"

—Cece McCauley

At first the social standards of Aklavik were carried over to the new community. For the closely knit settlement, any party or meeting was a get-together for everyone, from Administrator to construction worker. There was no distinct social hierarchy.

"Whenever the Catholic Women's League or the Anglican Women's League had a meeting or tea everyone went whether it was for them or not. Someone's feelings would have been hurt if they had been left out. Everybody mixed. It didn't make any difference what your colour or religion was."

—Dawn Zubko

It was a time in the new town when people were learning about each other and about the different cultural backgrounds everyone had come from. The new residents from southern Canada brought their own ideas on the establishment of social groups.

For established northerners and native people alike it was a mutual process of learning, a first exposure to community meetings. For many it was the first opportunity to be involved in the development of an organization from the grass roots level.

"We really kept busy in those days. We formed all these organizations – the Home and School and the Community Association. Mrs. "Dusty" Miller and Mrs. Holman were always involved. We got everything going. There was nothing here, remember."

—*Agnes Semmler*

Festivals and holidays were a time for the entire community to join together.

Christmas celebrations in Inuvik were not unlike those in any other Canadian town, with a couple of exceptions. There were no chimneys on the houses for Santa to climb down, and he did not use reindeer; he arrived instead on a sled pulled by a team of huskies!

Victor Allen was the town's first "Santa Claus." He made his debut in front of the school to a cheering throng of children.

"His dogs didn't want to run that day. Someone ran ahead of his team pulling at the dogs. What a sight! All the little children standing on the steps of the school shouting, 'Here comes Santa Claus!' and there was Santa with his dog team that didn't want to run. He made the children so happy."

—*Agnes Semmler*

Christmas was also a time when townspeople visited back and forth bearing gifts of homemade bread and Christmas treats. New Year's Eve was often celebrated with a drum dance, performed under the teepee-shaped dome at the Research Lab.

The winter months were a constant round of outdoor activities for Inuvik residents.

At winter carnival time there were dog-sled rides for the children. Herders from Reindeer Station would drive a few of their herd to town so the children could have a reindeer ride, just like their southern counterparts could enjoy a pony ride at the local fair.

Today in Inuvik festivals and winter sports abound. There are the Arctic Winter Games and the International Curling Bonspiels. There are figure skating championships. There is snowmobiling and, probably most popular of all, cross-country skiing.

There was even downhill skiing in Inuvik until a devastating fire destroyed the trees and terrain near the townsite.

"As a boy it was always my dream to be a downhill ski instructor. It never happened but when I came to Inuvik we thought we should have a ski hill. Some of us hooked up a tow rope on an old tractor wheel and powered it with a generator. We had the ski hill on the slope down the hill from the hospital. The kids really enjoyed that hill in those days."

—*Barney MacNeil*

The unique conception of Inuvik, as a model town in the far northern wilderness, fostered concern in some quarters about the vast socio-economic problems which might result.

The town was inundated with Ph.d's and scientists. Serious-minded studies were conducted on the people who reporters and authors interviewed continuously. Geophysical specialists studied the effects of habitation upon the Arctic landscape.

The residents of Inuvik endured wave after wave of government personnel armed with surveys and questionnaires. They were amused by the Anthropologists who followed them through their daily activities. They tolerated the photographers and film crews who descended to make innumerable documentaries. The subject families never saw the finished products, but this intensive period of study spawned a well-known Arctic joke:

Question: What is a normal Inuvik family?
Answer: Father, mother, child and anthropologist!

The children of Inuvik were especially adept at bridging cultural barriers, and were often a primary source of information for many of the studies of life in Inuvik. Indeed, it was the children who were always on hand as a welcoming party to the geologists who paddled down the river during the summer months.

This scrutinization process, which began in the early days, helped create Inuvik's social fabric. Many of those who came to the new town out of curiousity or scientific interest stayed on and made Inuvik their home. Their common background as "newcomers" served to draw the people together.

Shopping at Hudson's Bay store, Inuvik, circa. 1965

"When I first came here everyone still knew everybody else. There weren't that many people here yet. When the white people came they made friends with the natives. They were just like brothers and sisters."

—Catherine Mitchell

"We arrived just before Christmas one year. The thing I remember most was the hospitality of the people here who brought things to the house for Christmas. There was such a sense of being 'one' town."

—Cynthia Hill

There were only a few places where the people could meet or join in community activity. The school gymnasium was a popular meeting spot for organized activity as was the conference room at the Scientific Research Laboratory.

"There was no television in Inuvik at that time and Friday nights became 'movie night' at the Research Lab. Everyone enjoyed being able to see a movie."

—Dick Hill

The social spirit was very much alive. As trained technicians began to arrive from southern Canada they were welcomed into the social milieu along with longtime Delta residents. The whole town seemed to mingle freely.

"There was no television in those days. People socialized more. There always seemed to be Open House parties and everyone went. People from town came over to the mess functions as well. It was a warm, friendly atmosphere."

—CWO Russ Israel

"The first weekend I arrived in Inuvik in '62 Dave Anderson, who ran Tuk Traders, invited us to a party. Away we went in a single otter with Dave serving champagne! He seemed to capture the spirit of the place; for him life seemed to be one giant party."

—Jim Robertson

In the early days a sense of isolation from the rest of Canada and the world served to draw the townspeople together. There were no outside influences such as television, videotape recorders or video games. Radio was the single most important form of communication, and everyone got to participate.

"When you wanted to send a message you just walked down to the radio station. Someone there handed you the microphone and you did it live. I remember distinctly that most messages ended with the same words: 'As for myself, I am the same.'"

—Barney MacNeil

No one in Inuvik needed a journalism degree to be a broadcaster. Many people did have radio experience, but they had learned the hard way – by simply doing it.

"Everyone from Aklavik was a broadcaster. Over there the radio station was run by volunteers. It was your civic duty to go down and help out a couple of hours a week. Here in Inuvik it was the same. People came in to do volunteer work all the time."

—Nellie Cournoyea

THE ROYAL VISIT

Inuvik has been host to foreign ambassadors, prime ministers and diplomats, but its most famous visitors have been the Royal Family.

In 1970, the Queen, Prince Philip, Prince Charles and Princess Anne toured the Northwest Territories in celebration of its Centennial. When they arrived in Inuvik the townspeople were surprised but delighted that the Family was not surrounded by throngs of press recording the event. Inclement Arctic weather had delayed the press plane indefinitely in Tuktoyaktuk.

The townspeople lined the square in front of the elementary school hoping to shake hands and speak with the Queen.

Agnes Semmler was manager of the Inuvik Craft Shop at the time and remembers the Mounties in scarlet tunics arriving to inspect the premises before the Royal Family toured the shop, browsing and purchasing northern handicrafts.

The warm northern welcome extended to the Monarch was not all pomp and ceremony. It was tinged with a touch of humour. Dick Hill, Mayor of Inuvik at the time, remembers.

> *"One evening we had a reception and the Queen and Prince Philip were in separate rooms to give more people the opportunity to meet them. When Prince Philip entered the room where I thought the Queen was to be I blurted out that he was in the wrong room. He looked rather stunned. I didn't know the plans had been changed.*
>
> *The next morning we were walking together up the steps of the school to another reception. We arrived in front of all those doors and the Prince paused, looked at each door and turned to me: 'Now, be very specific,' he said, 'Which door would you like me to go in?'"*

—Dick Hill

Ferris wheel on barge during Centennial celebrations.

The people's sense of isolation was increased by poor shopping facilities and a scarcity of goods people in less remote places take for granted. The Hudson's Bay Company stocked fresh fruit and vegetables year round but the choice was extremely limited, and things were not necessarily fresh after long shipment from the south. Government personnel and the Canadian Forces base staff were encouraged to shop in bulk, and to have their orders shipped once a year by barge.

"There was a trend at the time to make bulk orders. The government offered A or B orders for single or married people. They would barge in a year's order at a time. We only did that once. You always ate all the meat and were left by the end of the year with cans and cans of beans. There just wasn't a good balance."

—*Dick Hill*

"From the base Canex delivered once a month. They would send around a list of groceries and you checked off what you wanted. You didn't always get it, though. There were never things like tuna or mayonnaise. You would get fresh fruit, but it might be 3 bananas one week and 5 apples the next."

—*Marie Israel*

Isolation probably increased the sense of community spirit in Inuvik. The remoteness of the town made dreamers of the most pragmatic men and women.

"The town was a vibrant place. It had then, and has retained a feeling of vitality and spirit. The excitement that continued to surround the whole town gives me the impression that this is a real, moving place. There was always the feeling amongst the people here that this is a 'frontier' that we are all in this together."

—*Jim Robertson*

Inuvik has pushed back a frontier.

Man had mastered the insurmountable difficulties of the environment. Houses had been built, and people were living in them. A sense of social unity pervaded the business and personal sectors of the town. Committees and organizations had been formed. People were achieving, opening businesses and making corporate decisions. And less than 15 years had passed since Inuvik was only a concept in the minds of bureaucrats in Ottawa.

Canada's Centennial year, 1967, was fast approaching. Inuvik's townspeople wanted to do something special to commemorate the occasion, something that would prove to the rest of Canada that there really *was* life north of the 60th. The town's Centennial Committee sifted through hundreds of suggestions, ideas, architectural drawings and written proposals. All were considered, many would be implemented.

The decision was made to build a museum and library, in order to preserve pioneer and aboriginal artifacts for future generations. The centennial project would be built to celebrate not only the country's birth. It was a monument to the creation of the Town of Inuvik itself.

On January 14, 1967, the Inuvik Centennial Library was officially opened. Today it is the only public library within the Arctic Circle.

The Library was the only major centennial project in the Northwest Territories to be completed in time to celebrate the opening of Canada's Centennial year.

It had been organized and designed by the people of Inuvik. It was financed by a Centennial grant and constructed by a local contractor, Mackenzie Delta Construction Company. From the moment the project was conceived until the last nail was driven home, it had taken less than six months.

For the people of Inuvik, it was another first.

There could be no doubt that they were meeting the challenge of urbanizing the Arctic.

PIONEERING BOOM
'In Search of Energy'

Oil companies had been exploring the Mackenzie Delta and Beaufort region since the late 1950s. Throughout the sixties and into the seventies, the Delta was criss-crossed by seismic teams looking for the riches hidden beneath the earth. But it was the events far to the west, along the same Arctic coast, that caught the imaginations of oil explorers who rushed into the area.

Oil was discovered at Prudhoe Bay, Alaska in March 1968. Almost overnight companies looking to make the same kind of strike in Canada moved in.

People began to talk about a pipeline to carry Prudhoe Bay oil across to the Mackenzie Delta, and then down to southern markets.

It was obvious that whatever happened in the Delta and Beaufort would greatly affect Inuvik.

After the Prudhoe discovery, the federal government received dozens of applications for land in the region. Lots were allocated on a first come-first serve basis.

Inuvik was quickly becoming the main staging point for the oil exploration. In a period of three weeks, the community received six inquiries for industrial and warehouse sites from oil exploration companies. Ben de Kleine, Village Secretary in those days, said one company executive told him, "Next year your town is going to be hit by something that will be beyond your wildest imaginings."

Imperial Oil struck oil at Atkinson Point in January of 1970. In later years it found natural gas at Taglu and Mallik. Gulf and Mobil also struck gas at Parsons Lake.

A longtime resident of Inuvik, remembers oil and gas exploration at that time.

"It had pretty well shut down around 1965 or 1966 when Rainbow Lake oil field (in northwestern Alberta) was discovered. Two weeks later everyone who was working here during that winter was gone! They stockpiled their equipment at certain locations and just took their expert personnel all out."
—*Mike Zubko*

Oil exploration and seismic work in the area abruptly shut down with news of the Rainbow Lake oil discovery. In two weeks, their equipment was moved to river banks for barge pickup and the crews hurried to pursue the major oil play in Alberta.

But when oil was found at Prudhoe Bay in 1968, the oil workers came back immediately.

Inuvik was bustling. There was an air of excitement, everybody saw the possibility of economic prosperity for the region.

The town was growing. The population had increased from 2,250 in 1967, to 3,080 in 1970. Steps were being taken to bring better housing, sewer and water facilities to the town's west end.

Construction of Inuvik's arena and recreation complex began in 1968. It was the idea of a number of community-minded people, especially Lieutenant Commander Larry Mann. The arena was paid for by a number of grants and donations of services and equipment. Volunteers helped the contractor erect the new facility.

The previous year the town had a new secondary school, opened by The Hon. Jean Chretien in October, 1967.

There was a good deal of controversy over what it should be named. The Federal government's policy was to name schools after northern explorers. The townspeople thought Inuvik's new school should be called Aneesaluk High School after a well-known and respected Inuit leader in the Western Arctic, Charlie Smith. His Inuvialuit name means "a going out from – as in a river entering the sea." They pointed out that the elementary school, Sir Alexander Mackenzie School, was already named after an explorer. One who was in the area only seven days, two hundred years ago. But the government won. The new high school was named after the explorer, Samuel Hearne.

Inuvik was attracting attention from more than oil companies. The Royal family, cabinet ministers, foreign diplomats, and celebrities like Anne Murray, Ian and Sylvia, the Irish Rovers, and Astronaut James Lovell, all came to visit.

The town caught "Trudeaumania" in August of 1968, shortly after Pierre Elliot Trudeau was elected Prime Minister. He stepped from a DC-3 at Inuvik's airstrip to be greeted by a troupe of curious residents. He mingled with the crowd, and bestowed a few kisses – the first one to Matilda McNeill. After a tour of the town, he settled into Grollier Hall and waited for dinner.

(Continued page 50)

Delta Drum Dancer

MONA THRASHER

Mona Thrasher, Inuvik's renowned artist, lives in a small red house behind the "Igloo Church". She has not been able to speak or hear since the age of 13 when a shotgun blast left her partially deaf and mute.

Mona communicates through her paintings illustrating scenes from her childhood in the Delta and the Eskimo life of her forefathers.

Her beginnings as an artist coincide with the building of the Our Lady of Victory Church. Mona was 18 when Father Joseph Adam asked her to paint the stations of the cross that adorn the circular walls of the church today.

The parish now has a permanent collection of a dozen of Mona's finest pieces housed in the adjacent small Family Hall.

Mona is a prolific artist, painting up to 40 oils a year and in 1982 she began using pastels.

Father Denis Croteau, the present pastor of the church, estimates that Mona has created over 1000 pieces of work which have been sold throughout Canada and the United States.

An Arctic Wild Rose

Aerial view of Aklavik – the community that wouldn't die

Sun glows on the winter horizon

First stockpile of lumber awaits construction at the new site of East Three (1954)

Aerial view of the site (summer 1955)

Road construction begins (summer 1955)

The Schooner "Messenger" arrives from Aklavik with new residents for East Three

East end of Distributor Street-first "residential" section at East Three

Government Garage under construction

"512's" soon to be the Anglican Mission at the new site

East Four site – airport construction crew removes gravel to be used as fill

The site grows as construction continues

Stringer Hall under construction. The Hostel will be home from September to June for children from remote settlements while they attend school

The Midnight summer sun reflects on the water in the wake of a fishing boat

December 21st and − 45°. The winter sun reflects on the clouds but will not rise until early January

*u.r.: cross-section of utilidor
system developed to carry
sewage, water and heat.*

*l.l.: R.C.M.P. buildings in
background. Markers for
original C.B.C. building in
foreground.*

*l.r.: Fred Norris's barge and tug
in background. D.P.W. dock
facility downstream.*

First school in a ''512'' on Distributor Street

ANGLICAN
MISSION
REGULAR SERVICES
• 1:30 SUNDAY SCHOOL
• 2:30 UNUM KENGAOTAIT
• 7:00 EVENING PRAYER

"Jesus Christ the same yesterday,
and to-day, and forever" –
Hebrews 13:8
YOU ARE WELCOME

Anglican Mission opens in 1957

Ice fog retreats across the river as the sun peeps over the winter horizon in early January ending the long weeks of darkness

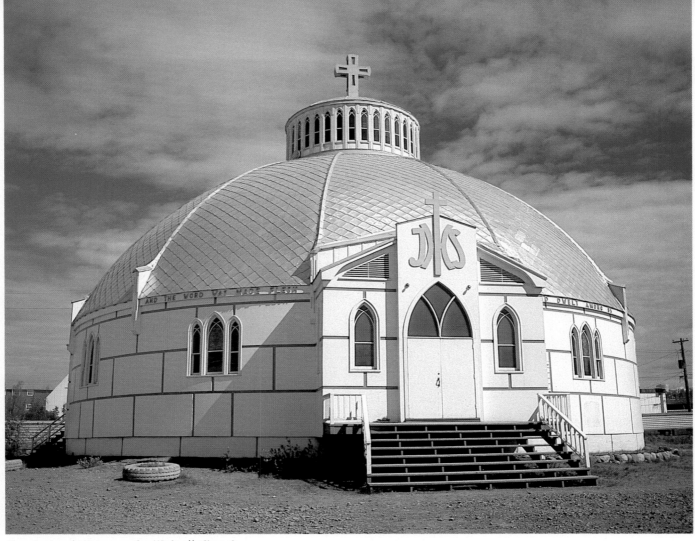

Our Lady of Victory – the "Igloo" Church

Northern lights dance in the winter sky over the Church in a painting by Mona Thrasher

Painting by Mona Thrasher hangs in the Igloo Church

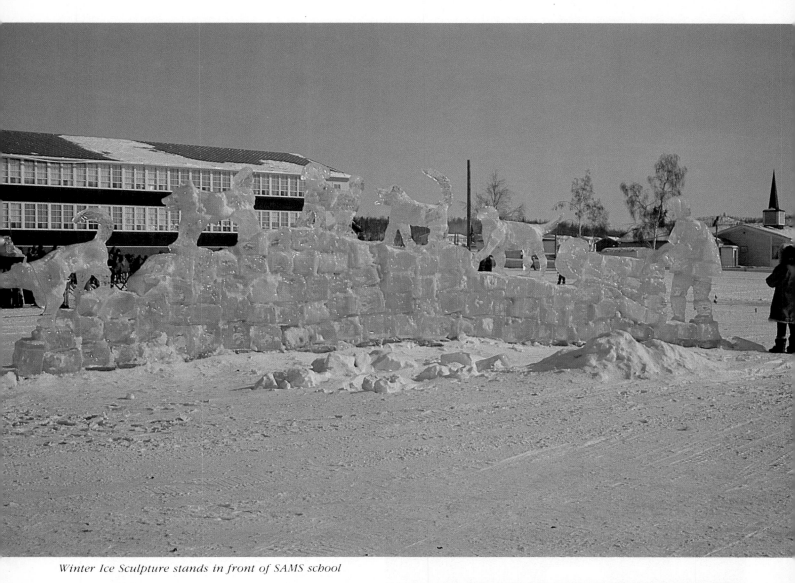

Winter Ice Sculpture stands in front of SAMS school

Beautiful handcrafts adorn the walls of Ingamo Hall during the craft festival held each autumn

*Northern Games, 1970 –
Bannock making – Ellen Abels
and Frannie Charlie*

Northern Games, 1970 – Loucheux Indians – fellowship around the tea pot

Magnificent view on the Dempster Highway (below Tombstone)

THE DEMPSTER HIGHWAY

On warm summer evenings the residents of Inuvik often stroll through Happy Valley campground checking licence plates of the tourists' vehicles.

The campground is the final destination of tourists who have travelled the 700 km gravel road of the Dempster from Dawson City, Yukon.

Other than those who drive the highway in pickups, campers, and mobile homes there are those who venture up it by hitchiking, bicycling, jogging and in the winter, by dogsled.

The highway gets its name from Inspector W. J. D. Dempster of the Northwest Mounted Police. He was instrumental in locating the "lost patrol" – four Mounties who died on the trek between Ft. McPherson, N.W.T. and Dawson City, Yukon in the winter of 1910-1911.

The Dempster Highway, officially opened in 1979, culminated a 20 year old dream of the Hon. John G. Diefenbaker who envisioned a road "to the Arctic".

That evening the PM walked into the kitchen and casually addressed the cook, Clara Phillips, "What's for dinner?"

The cook, not recognizing the Prime Minister, answered sarcastically, "Muktuk and boiled rabbit!"

"Good," replied the PM, and sauntered out again.

It is not known if he was disappointed with the actual main course of fried chicken, roast prime rib, peas, marquis potatoes and a fresh tossed salad from Father Adam's garden.

Oil and gas exploration of the region continued on a massive scale. After the Prudhoe Bay discovery, expenditures by fuel companies doubled in one year – from 30 to 60 million dollars. With significant discoveries of natural gas in the delta, there was more talk of a pipeline to carry the gas south.

It was said a pipeline would mean an expenditure of several billion dollars and employ 5,500 people during the construction stages, plus 150 in the maintenance and operating stages.

By 1973, 66 wells had been drilled in the lower Mackenzie area and on Richards Island. Imperial, Shell and Gulf had all made significant discoveries. But the most important finds were on the seaward edge of the Delta. It appeared that even bigger discoveries could be found offshore.

The increase in exploration brought an increase in jobs.

Freddie Carmichael, a pilot born in Aklavik, says he remembers flying over the land at night and seeing nothing but lights from the seismic camps.

Events were changing the native way of life. In 1968, Reindeer Station was closed down. The Canadian Wildlife Service had taken over the Northwest Territories Reindeer Project. The 20 families that lived on the Delta to look after the herd were moved – with their houses.

Some found the change difficult to accept.

"I sure didn't want to move to Inuvik at that time, boy," he says. "I sure didn't but what could we do? We had to go with the houses. We had no choice. We had to make a living too. Inuvik was hard for kids. We had seven kids then and they were small and they didn't know anything about the road. Our house was on the road, and they had to learn about the traffic."

—*Jimmy Gordon*

Prime Minister Trudeau at Inuvik airport, 1970

Gordon says the people in Inuvik weren't that much different – he just missed Reindeer Station. But he has a home in Inuvik now, and wouldn't want to move back.

But while some things were in danger of being lost, others were being strengthened.

In the late sixties there was a concerted effort to retain and promote northern traditional sports and skills. The skills existed, but weren't being passed on to young people.

The Mackenzie Delta Drummers and Dancers were established. Billy Day of Inuvik helped organize drum dancers from Aklavik, Tuktoyaktuk and Inuvik. The group of old-timers were a big hit not only in the North but in southern Canada as well. In 1970, they performed at the first Arctic Games before the Prime Minister. Shortly after they performed for the Royal Family. In 1971 they won the Drum Dancing championship at the World Eskimo Olympics at Fairbanks, Alaska.

Nellie Cournoyea, a native rights activist in the Western Arctic, remembers that during the Canadian Centennial many people wondered why native culture in the North wasn't promoted more. Ms. Cournoyea says that many of the Northern sports have always been popular, but only recently have they become organized and high-profile.

In 1969, plans were made for the Arctic Winter Games to be held in Yellowknife. Many people were unhappy that these games would include only southern sports, like basketball and hockey. That year, under the chairmanship of Edward Lennie of Inuvik, a group was formed to look into holding a celebration of truly Northern games in the summer of 1970. Lennie researched the skills from old-timers and organized the Inuvik Northern Games team.

The first games were held in Inuvik as part of the Centennial of the Northwest Territories. They were a great success, and have since become an annual event.

Fourteen communities participated during the first year, hailing from as far west as Point Barrow, in Alaska, and as far east as Coppermine. Never meant to be a competitive athletic contest, the Northern Games have always been more like a Northern festival, where native people can get together and exchange their skills. Some of these skills include the high kick, the one-hand reach, the blanket toss, and "good woman" events, such as tea boiling, seal and muskrat skinning, duck plucking and bannock making.

Native people were also excelling in non-traditional sports. The Firth twins, Shirley and Sharon, were beginning to make waves on the international cross-country ski circuit.

The Firths made their debut as a result of the Territorial Experimental Ski Training – or TEST program. The TEST program was established in 1967 to see if a cross-country ski program could be set up that would motivate native young people to become competitive and high-achieving athletes. It was hoped that active sports participation would give them the self-esteem they needed to become high achievers in school and in the employment world as well.

Rigorous training and world-class coaching paid off. In the first year of the TEST program, Fred Kelly won the Canadian Junior Championships, and the Inuvik girls won the first five spots in their category at the same meet. At the U.S. Junior Nationals in Montana, Shirley Firth – who was then only 14 – came in first. Her sister Sharon was third.

In the next few years, the team did well in meets across Europe, and in Sapporo, Japan where the Firths and Lorraine Bullock competed in the 1972 Olympics, but failed to place. Later many of the skiers dropped out of international competition. But the Firths remain today as a source of pride and inspiration for many young Northerners.

The TEST program's first professional coach, Bjorger Pettersen, set up the first Top of the World Ski Championship in Inuvik 16 years ago. It gave TEST skiers a chance to ski against international class racers. When Coach Pettersen left the team, the calibre of this meet changed. Today the emphasis is on fun and recreation, and getting the outlying communities involved.

Peggy Curtis, a physical education teacher at the time of the TEST program, felt the program dropped off from more than just the lack of rigorous coaching.

"The social fibre of the community changed in those years as well. There are more things for kids to do today. It's easier to stay at home and watch TV than go out skiing, work up a sweat and freeze."
—*Peggy Curtis*

That "changing social fibre" was noticed by many people. In the late sixties, more and more native people began to worry about the effects of exploration on the land and their way of life. Many of them wanted reassurance that development would bring prosperity for native people as well as whites.

Agnes Semmler was president of the first native association to be established in the Arctic. The inaugural meeting was held in January, 1970. It included a spectrum of people: Inuvialuit, Dene, Metis, and concerned white people.

"What really started us off was Richard Rohmer. He had two big plane loads of people and they were going to Tuk to look over the situation and see where they suspected oil to be. He got me to show them around and Mary Teddie (Joe Teddie's wife) to go with the other plane and show them around."

"We took them to Tuk and they were looking over the land. They were waiting in the plane and saying if there was any oil to be found, they would find it in Tuk. Rohmer told us that we should start something, so we could get in on this oil deal."
—*Agnes Semmler*

That "something" became the Committee for Original People's Entitlement (COPE).

"On parade", Northern Games, 1970, Inuvik

There was no money for the native group at the beginning. Before long it turned over its membership in Coppermine and farther east to the newly formed Inuit Tapirisat. Soon the Indian Brotherhood (now the Dene Nation) and the Metis Association took over land rights negotiations for the Dene.

With the increased talk of a pipeline to take natural gas south from the Delta, there was an urgency to settle land claims with the federal government.

Sam Raddi became involved with COPE after it was established. He felt COPE could not endorse a pipeline while there were people afraid of the effects of exploration on the land and wildlife. There were reports of dead fish in lakes passed through by seismic explorers setting off dynamite. The group was in close contact with the native people in Alaska, who were already experiencing the effects of a pipeline from the Prudhoe Bay discovery.

COPE would have a lot to say during the Berger inquiry.

But that was only one part of COPE's activities. It was also involved in the first Northern Games, native radio broadcasting, and various native organizations including the Inuvik Housing Co-operative and Namaktok Limited, a corporation established to help native people set up businesses. Those early years were exciting ones for COPE.

Agnes Semmler

Bertha Allen

"Everything was brand new. It was just a lot of fun. You know, learning politics, meeting people, going to meetings for the first time. It was tough in a way, yet it was fun. I think it's fun to learn. All of us were the same, we were all learning. We laughed at each other sometimes, too."

—*Sam Raddi*

In a space of a few years, Inuvik moved closer to the outside world and lost some of its isolation. There had been telephones in town for several years, but it wasn't until August 2, 1966 that people could telephone friends and relatives down south. On that summer night the townspeople crowded into the gymnasium of SAMS school and waited breathlessly while the inaugural long distance call was made.

"We all gathered at the school in the gym and they said that they were going to talk to some people down south. And that's what they did. I couldn't believe it! I thought they were just making it up! People were talking on the phone all the way from down south to here. I remember sitting there listening to them and thinking that it was just somebody else in the building talking. I didn't believe that it had come from far away."

—*Catherine Mitchell*

The long distance telephone had advantages and disadvantages. Before the phone link telex was the only contact with the south. After that summer night utility bills sky-rocketed as everyone tried the new service.

The string of telephone poles and cable was a big white elephant.

"The phones weren't very reliable because a strong wind could bring the whole system down. I remember an operator telling me one day, that the phones were out because a moose had its antlers caught in the telephone wires!"

—*Dawn Zubko*

The telephone land line was replaced with the microwave communication system used today.

Television came to Inuvik in the form of three week-old videotape packages in 1969. Live television didn't arrive until 1973.

Jimmy Gordon remembers buying a television when the frontier packages were still being shown. It was a few weeks late, but the first thing he watched that night was an astronaut taking his first steps on the moon.

Now there were complete communications with the rest of Canada and the world. People living in Inuvik could pick up a phone and dial south, get on a jet and step off in Edmonton in a matter of hours, or turn on the television and watch world events as they happened.

Inuvik grew in population and physical size with the affluence of oil and gas exploration. The airport was expanded, and a control tower built in 1972. Inuvik had its first jet link to the south with Pacific Western Airlines 737 service.

New businesses sprang up. Alex and Nan Foreman opened another grocery store in town. Simpsons-Sears opened a catalogue outlet. A new building was opened downtown that housed the Ravens Nest restaurant, Mac's News Stand, Rexall Drugs and a bar called the Mad Trapper.

The Mad Trapper developed a special appeal for the transient population of Inuvik. People leaving town traditionally tack their "last buck" to the Trapper's wall. Someday when they come back, they'll still have a dollar for a beer. It's an optimistic tradition, in that it predicts that all who drink there will someday return to Inuvik and still be able to buy a drink for only a dollar!

There was a lot of money and optimism in Inuvik during those oil boom days, with several companies confident of the natural gas reserves in the Mackenzie Delta, others starting to look to the Beaufort Sea, and almost everyone sure that a pipeline would be built.

"Things were moving really fast. There were times when you could go away for a two or three month holiday, then come back to find that the whole town had changed. I remember I came back once to discover my neighbourhood had moved
away, lock, stock and barrel. Three houses that had been adjacent to mine were all moved. One had gone 30 or 40 feet back to the utilidor and the others were just gone."
—Dan Holman

Many people in Inuvik were busy working, and dreaming.

These dreams however almost went up in smoke in August, 1968 when the young town of Inuvik was threatened by a bush fire. Before it was brought under control, the blaze had four days to devour trees and tundra over a huge area. Smoke could be seen for 80 km or more, and wind-driven ashes fell as far away as Aklavik, 60 km to the west.

The entire town mobilized to fight the threat. The people of Inuvik pulled together with volunteers from Aklavik and the surrounding Delta. Many residents have sharply etched memories of that dangerous time.

"I was working at the hospital. When I got there in the morning the night nurse saw the smoke way up at the garbage dump. She asked the RCMP about it and was told it was nothing. When she looked again she saw flames. The fire got bigger and they had to fight it that day. High winds made it spread fast. There was lots of smoke."
—Catherine Mitchell

"Wilf Taylor was the lands and forests officer, and he took charge. The town could have caught fire. The blaze had to be controlled so it didn't get into the town. There was an Emergency Measures plan and the Research Lab was made the operations centre for fire control. It was decided that the bars would be closed, and all available men put out to the fire line. It was fascinating to see the men come streaming out. The scheduling of everything, feeding people, transporting them, went on for four days."
—Dick Hill

Despite the urgency of the situation, there were lighter moments.

"The men who were out fighting the fire saw a bear, and they were more afraid of the bear than they were of the fire. All these men started running away from the bear on the road. The bear passed them and just kept on going. He was more afraid of the fire than they were."
—Agnes Semmler

Main street, Inuvik, 1972

Hudson's Bay store, Inuvik, 1972

Semmler's General Store - watching a Delta Daze Parade, 1980

"Slim" Semmler inside his general store, East Three's original store

RCMP headquarters, Inuvik, circa. 1965

"Probably the most exciting time was when the fire got to the military base outside of Inuvik. Although they had their own Emergency Measures plan, they didn't think the grass was as thick as it was. All their buildings were steel. But they were set on wooden pilings and the piles burned away and the masts fell down. This was a military embarrassment. When the Russians come all they'd have to do is start a grass fire!"

—*Dick Hill*

Plans made to evacuate the town were fortunately never used but it was a fearful time for many.

*"One day they said that **everybody** had to go to fight the fire. The boys and men were there and the girls were serving sandwiches. That night it was dark and you could see the flames, and I was really afraid. I'm not ashamed to say it. I just went and knelt down and I really prayed for rain – prayed and prayed for rain. It seemed like it started raining and it really poured, and after that the fire was out."*

—*Catherine Mitchell*

The close call pulled the people of Inuvik together as they never had been before. Everyone worked to face the common danger, and everybody shared what they had.

"We were living on Co-Op Hill then. We had to move out of our house because there were a lot of trees around, and we moved to the centre of town. I was really scared because I thought we would never be able to go back to our house. We stayed with the Hills until the fire was out."

—*Shirley Allen Kisoun*

"They just made up their minds they could all work together. From that time on I have always tried to get people working together because I know they can. There's no such thing as "can't".

—*Edward Lennie*

As the threat from the devastating fire retreated, a renewed community spirit emerged.

The townspeople returned to their growing businesses. Dreams of the future developments and prosperity continued.

The social fabric of the town, which had been fused in the fight to save their homes would be tested in the turbulent years to come. It would not be found wanting.

Father Joseph Adam in front of "Igloo Church" under construction, 1959

Construction of the inside dome of the Church

The Church today

THE
IGLOO CHURCH

Our Lady of Victory Church, the "Igloo Church", is Inuvik's most famous tourist attraction.

The church is the only major building in the town not built on wooden pilings. It rests on a gravel pad with a small stream running underneath, causing skeptics to quip that only divine intervention prevents the church from sinking into the permafrost.

Two Roman Catholic missionaries, Brother Maurice Larocque and Father Joseph Adam, collaborated to design a church which would reflect the uniqueness of the people it serves. The igloo shape represents not only the idea of a shelter but the inside dome of an igloo has an Inuvialuktun name meaning "sky" and is associated with spiritual aspiration.

There were no blueprints. The plans were in Brother Larocque's head.

The two men had gravel transported by barge from Point Separation. The gravel was then laid two metres thick into a saucer-like depression. A concrete rim was poured on top and an outer shell of the dome was erected. A second dome was built inside – its 12 wooden arches representing the Apostles.

The space between the two domes would serve as a heat exchanger.

The church took two years to complete and in August, 1960 "Our Lady of Victory Church" opened its doors.

Children on the "Diefenbaker" monument in front of the elementary school, 1962

THE YEARS OF CHANGE
'Reflections After Berger'

A time of social change and excitement, and of national interest in the people of the North, was heralded in the 1970s by the government's hearings about the social and environmental implications of a pipeline through the Mackenzie Valley.

Some called it Justice Tom's Flying Circus. Officially it was the Mackenzie Valley Pipeline Inquiry. Most knew it plainly as the Berger Commission.

Almost 10 years after it was created people still talk about the B.C. Supreme Court Judge, the two years of Canada-wide hearings and the effect made by one man's decision in 1977.

As Inuvik and the rest of the North reconsiders Beaufort oil and gas development in the 1980s, there is a definite sense of "deja vu"; we've been through this before. Inuvik's vitality was linked with the outcome of Berger's report; it is tied to decisions about the Beaufort undersea resources.

Tom Berger was commissioned on March 21, 1974 to investigate the potential effects of building a gas pipeline along the Mackenzie River Valley.

There were two proposals. Canadian Arctic Gas wanted to transport Alaskan gas from Prudhoe Bay across the Northern Yukon to a Mackenzie Valley pipeline. Foothills Pipelines would carry Canadian gas from fields in the Delta directly south along the same route.

It was more than just a pipeline proposal for natural gas. The assumption was always that an oil pipeline would follow, then eventually roads, a railroad, power lines and telecommunications, creating a transportation and energy corridor.

Berger's was the first inquiry to really examine the impact of development on the environment, the economy and the people. From the formal technical hearings in large centres, Berger took his crew to small settlements by bush plane to listen to the people speak – often in their native language. He visited every community in the Western Arctic between April 1975 and August 1976.

Berger came to Inuvik twice in early 1976. At times nearly 300 people crammed Family Hall. Many spoke. Berger just listened.

"It was the first time lots of people ever saw a judge talking about land. They were a little embarrassed."

—*Ishmael Alunik*

"People were shyer then. – But we would sponsor them and people would go there and give testimony."

—*Sam Raddi*

Lois Ross remembers that the native people liked Berger. "He tried to make the hearings informal so that people had a minimum of discomfort."

He was not, however, popular with many of the established white people in the North. Some people felt his politics were just a little too apparent. He'd been leader of the NDP party in British Columbia and at the time of his appointment the NDP held the balance of power in the House of Commons.

At the hearings the justice heard variations on three themes, build, don't build, build with conditions.

Jim Robertson presented the town's position. He had been acclaimed mayor early in 1973, taking over from L. P. Holman.

The town favoured controlled development. It supported a quick settlement to land claims and jobs for Northerners.

Among the most eloquent speakers at the Inuvik hearings was Ellen Binder, who had been involved with COPE and had sat on town council. She talked of how easy it was to be labelled pro or anti-development.

"Things aren't that simple...there should be a cooling-off period to allow people to adjust, advance their training and further the necessary research. The people must be given a chance to determine their own future. Care should be taken not to get carried away by emotion and lose perspective on life."

—*Ellen Binder*

Modern apartments at Inuvik standing high above the ground on their "stilts", September, 1981

But many people were afraid. They were afraid of blowouts. They were afraid the caribou would leave. They were afraid there would be no jobs for their children and no compensation for their land.

"It was fear of the unknown," says Sam Raddi. People didn't trust the oil companies, because they remembered their past experiences with seismic crews.

For those who were directly involved, waiting for Berger's recommendations was an intense, exciting, and often very confusing time. For the majority of people life just went on: Don and Claire Bowering had the first baby of 1976, a girl named Jeannette. Ed Broadbent came to town, as did the Belgian prime minister and Governor-General and Madame Leger.

An Inuvik doctor made international headlines. Angelo di Stefano, chief surgeon at the Inuvik General Hospital for nearly two years, was called a fake, picked up on an Interpol warrant by RCMP and deported to Italy. Although trained as a surgeon in the 50s, he left Italy before receiving his papers in order to avoid arrest for taking part in a student demonstration at the University of Rome. In Inuvik he did more than 300 operations, saving many lives. He was eventually cleared by the Italian courts and came back to Ontario.

When Berger left Inuvik to hold meetings in Tuktoyaktuk he asked Marie McInnes to come along. Marie had come North in the late 30s to live with her husband Mac at Reindeer Station. She moved to Inuvik in 1959 when Mac came to run the liquor store. When the Inquiry came to town, Marie made their coffee and took their phone messages.

"I don't like just coffee or tea by itself, so I started making squares and things. One of the Commission secretaries wanted to know why I did all that. Then she grabbed a bowl and put 50 cents in it. She told the rest of them, 'if you people want sweets, please donate.' At the end of that first day I had made about $7.00. I think what they liked best was the fact that I used to put a bottle of aspirin on their table in the morning."

—Marie McInnes

In 1974 the Inuvik business community had been riding an optimistic wave. The federal government encouraged the town to plan for expansion. The government itself started a $2 million addition to the hospital. The airport road was widened. The Northern Canada Power Commission made plans to expand its fuel storage.

The next year the town joined the building boom. Ingamo Hall was begun, as well as the town office building. A third floor was added to the Mack Travel building and Northern Canada Power Commission put a new water tank at Hidden Lake. The town had planned for double its current population (4200 at peak in 1972). It had borrowed $2 million from the territorial government to put in 170 serviced lots in the west end. (That meant clearing the land, laying gravel pads and extending the utilidor.)

But by 1976, people were beginning to get nervous. The town passed a "no development budget", even though gravel trucks still stirred up the dust on Mackenzie Road as they hauled loads to where new industries were expected to locate.

Mayor Robertson told the Edmonton Journal in June that he felt betrayed by the federal government. "It doesn't seem to be able to make up its mind on what's going on in the North. Berger isn't helping. No one expected the inquiry to run for two years.

If there's no pipeline," the mayor predicted, "the town will shrink to its size of 10 years ago."

On May 9, 1977, Mayor Robertson had even less reason to be pleased as the long-awaited Berger Inquiry report was released.

Under the title "Northern Frontier, Northern Homeland" Berger recommended a 10 year moratorium on development to give native organizations time to settle land claims. The delay would also give industry time to do more research. According to Berger, the North Yukon route should not be used because of the richness and sensitivity of the environment. He suggested it be made a national wilderness park.

Berger didn't say no to a gas pipeline. He saw one as both feasible and inevitable. But he wanted to ensure that such a pipeline would go ahead only after careful planning and under strict regulation.

Mainstreet, Inuvik

Les Carpenter was born in Fort McPherson and was a teenager in Sachs Harbour when the hearings were held. Like so many students who grew up in the hostel, he calls Inuvik home. After Berger, a whole new way of life emerged for the native people.

"All of a sudden the native organizations came into the limelight. People were signing up...people were 'born-again' natives...people were going back on the land. The oil companies were in limbo."
—Les Carpenter

The only bright time for those who favoured development was when Dome sailed its first two drillships into the Beaufort Sea, during the summer of 1976. Sun Oil had its first, and the season's only, oil find at Garry Island. Several step-out wells were drilled but no other new formations were found.

After Berger's report, Foothills Pipelines closed its Inuvik office. The company moved to Whitehorse to concentrate on promoting the "Alcan" pipeline route, along the Alaska Highway. Shell Oil announced it was pulling out. Gulf reported it was cutting back. And Dome looked like the only game in town.

"After the first part of the Berger report came out, the writing was on the wall. The town just went into shock," says Dan Holman. He had just taken over as editor/publisher of the Drum. Tom Butters had started the paper in the 60s but had moved to territorial politics in 1975 with his election as Inuvik's MLA.

"Businesses went bankrupt and people left. It hasn't recovered to this day, despite what's happened in the Beaufort," says Holman. "It's as tentative today as it was then."

Ex-mayor Cynthia Hill remembers there were a lot of people who came to Inuvik and positioned themselves for development. "Those people went away. The people who were here before, stayed. The community went on."

Her husband Dick Hill, calls the time after Berger the catching-up period. "Things really depended on the stabilizing influence of the long time residents. You'd start scratching around for something again. Not much by our own doing, the tourist industry started to develop."

PWA had developed a jet service during the oil days and in 1977 Midnight Sun Tours advertised airfare from Edmonton to Inuvik at $199, return.

The midnight sun was quite a novelty to southerners. The sun came up on May 24 and would not dip below the horizon again until July 19. It's always a crazy time of year, affecting people in strange ways. Some people complain they can't sleep because the sun is streaming through their windows at midnight. Others, especially the kids, seem to require little or no sleep. You can see their energy increase with the lengthening of the days.

Inuvik's number one tourist attraction is "Our Lady of Victory" – the Igloo Church. Father Denis Croteau entertains dozens of visitors daily during the summer with tours of the church and slide shows about the North.

In 1978 many people believed Inuvik was bottoming out. Several businesses closed their doors. The town's population dropped to 3200. The "Drum" could only afford to print an edition every other week. To keep everyone out of the pits of despair, the newspaper started a new column.

Editor Holman encouraged his readers to snitch on their friends and to share embarassing moments, like backing out of driveways into snowbanks or sliding around corners into the ditch. They could call their stories in to his telephone answering machines. The column, called "In The Ditch", awarded weekly points for the most creative winter driving. At the end of the season the points were tallied and the coveted Golden Shovel Award (sponsored by a local towing company) was presented to the red-faced winner. The column has gone on to become an institution.

The Drum also began a Ten Worst Dressed Men contest. Mutterings were heard that the editor himself should have headed the first winner's list.

1978 was also the year Inuvik's pirate television station, EVTV, went on the air.

The Dempster Highway Management Plan was released. Reaction was mixed. The mayor felt the impact of the highway could be more devastating than that of any pipeline. But others looked to the Dempster for tourism opportunities.

For COPE, 1978 was a good year. Land Claim negotiations with the federal government had moved along quickly. According to negotiator Nellie Cournoyea, the southern climate was in COPE's favour. "The economy was in better shape then than it is today. People were more generous: they could afford to be."

In October, at Sachs Harbour, an agreement in principle was signed. A final agreement was expected to follow in the next few months.

Inuvik was entering a reflective period. No longer was it the centre of national attention.

The new phase of community life was characterized by the town's new mayor, Cynthia Hill, an adult educator whose style was more cautious than that of her dynamic predecessor. Mrs Hill stressed planning, community involvement and public awareness during her four years of office.

Inuvik's main street was eventually paved. The wooden sidewalks that had served to keep mud and rubber boots from mixing during spring and autumn thaws, were put to rest. Tourists discovered Inuvik was more than a dot on a map after driving the Dempster Highway in its first season. A new town plan was prepared. A balanced budget was brought in, due largely to the territorial government's forgiving of the big boom debt. And the town studied a mini-gas pipeline from Parson's Lake as an alternate fuel source to the Northern Canada Power Commission.

Wooden cabins in west end of town

Fireweed Studios - a northern crafts studio owned by Dave and Myrna Button

NCPC is a troubled crown corporation, and Inuvik's source of freshwater, light and heat, except for those few households not hooked up to the utilidor. It is also Inuvik's favourite target for criticism.

"You always know when winter has really set in in Inuvik, because that's when the lights start to flicker."

—Dan Holman

In November 1982, a fire broke out in NCPC's main powerhouse. Fortunately the generators were unharmed, but for several hours that night, manager Jim Greenwood recalled a similar time three years earlier when a string of equipment breakdowns at NCPC had knocked out almost all of Inuvik's reserve generating power. It was November and -45°F. It took a week for an emergency generator to be shipped from Yellowknife, and meanwhile power had to be rotated between different parts of town. "Brownouts" were frequent. There was talk of evacuation, which never happened, but the situation was serious. It took a good two months for all the repairs to be made.

Afterwards there was a huge public outcry and both the Town and the Public Utilities Board investigated. But the experience was valuable and helped Inuvik residents to take the NCPC blackout of 1979 in stride.

Soon after the exciting progress of 1978, negotiations had begun to deteriorate on the COPE land claims. Change in governments, from Liberal to Conservative and back again, slowed things down.

Talks broke off completely in early 1981 and didn't reopen again until late 1982. During the lull, COPE turned its attention inward. A health study was commissioned. An ambitious research project to revitalize the Eskimo language was begun.

Times improved for the 600 Dene (Indian) and Metis people of Inuvik. The government had not taken seriously the Dene Declaration of 1975, which asserted the Dene and Metis right to be recognized as a separate nation.

The Dene had come to Inuvik from various bands, and fit into no category for funding from the federal government. They formed a loose association in 1977. But this Dene Council had no real voice.

In the spring of 1980, the Council decided to make a real effort to gain band status. They elected a Metis businesswoman to lead the fight.

Cece McCauley was only the third woman in Canada ever to be made a chief. Through her persistence and persuasive powers, the Inuvik Dene Band won full status in August 1982. Within two months the band assumed partnership in its first joint venture with Northern Metallic Sales, a major industrial supplier to the oil patch.

Cece has endless energy and endless plans. Big ones. "I want millions, not peanuts."

She wants to re-open Stringer Hall, standing empty since 1975. She wants to build an Olympic size swimming pool. She wants to create more job-training opportunities for her people. She looks to government and the oil companies to ensure these benefits for the Dene.

CBC on location at the riverbank for "breakup". Chuck Hendrie (CBC) interviews children, 1982

View of the Inuvik Marina, July, 1982

Midnight Sun reflects on the water, July, 1982

View of downtown businesses, main street, Inuvik

Despite the Berger report, drilling activity in the Beaufort Sea went steadily on, although there were some cutbacks. There were oil discoveries at Kopanoar, Tarsuit and Koakoak.

Imperial Oil concentrated on its artificial island building program, completing Issungnak. Dome enlarged its fleet to four drillships. But the sea ice formed early in 1980, shutting down operations in late October.

That month, the federal government announced a national energy program with generous incentives for frontier oil and gas exploration. Dome Petroleum was among the first companies to take advantage of the Canadian ownership clause; Dome Canada was formed early in the new year to handle the company's Beaufort Sea operations.

Throughout 1981, there was a definite sense that things were looking up again for business. In January the federal Environment Minister, John Roberts, approved the Norman Wells oil field expansion and pipeline. That July, Northern Affairs Minister John Munro asked Roberts to set up an environmental review of possible production and transportation of oil and gas from the Beaufort. The three major players, Dome, Esso and Gulf, collaborated to prepare an environmental impact statement. It was seven volumes long and a foot thick when it was finished over a year later.

Delta House opened in the old YMCA building after a $30,000 facelift. The community alcohol rehabilitation program looked permanent for the first time since its founding.

The Polaris Theatre closed after 18 years as Inuvik's only public movie house. Owners Glenn and Carole Bennett said high costs and competition with movies on video and satellite channels put them out of business.

CBC went on strike for four months over the summer. Some listeners complimented the picketers on management's programming, calling it a breath of fresh air.

As old friends and ski buddies stood proudly by, cross-country skiing stars Sharon and Shirley Firth were presented with the Commissioner's Award for outstanding achievement during the 14th annual Top of the World Ski Championships.

That year Dome doubled its spending in the Beaufort, to $400 million. It expanded its fleet again and com-

pleted a major building program at its base camp in Tuk. Gulf announced it planned to build a camp there, too.

Along with several other delta and coastal communities, Inuvik considered getting into a partnership agreement with Dome. But rumours started to filter through from Calgary that Dome was in big trouble with the banks. This was confirmed in September, 1982, when the federal government announced a half-billion dollar bailout scheme.

Local holders of Dome shares were seething. They'd watched their stock drop steadily after being issued. In March 1981, 80,000 shares had gone on sale in the North at $10 each, and were sold out in two weeks.

Marie McInnes was only one of many townspeople who sank money into the shares. A Dome official later advised her to hang onto her shares.

"He said they weren't going down forever. I wasn't too badly off. The people who borrowed money to buy the stocks, were harder up than I was. They had to pay the bank!"

—*Marie McInnes*

Dome Canada hit an all time low and trimmed its operation, but the company is still betting on the Beaufort.

As if to reflect the renewed activity of 1982, Jim Robertson stood again for election to the mayor's job and defeated Cynthia Hill.

At the beginning of 1983, Inuvik looked ahead to a year when Inuvialuit land claims would likely be settled, and major environmental hearings into Beaufort development would begin.

No one expects another Berger report to emerge from the hearings. It seems more likely that in some form, development of Arctic resources will be approved, and Inuvik is ready for the day that happens.

It's a cosmopolitan town, an up-to-date part of the Global Village, waiting on the edge of the largest development project the world has seen.

THE MOSQUITO MENACE

"They sit on telephone poles and drink out of ditches."
—Dan Holman

Northern residents complain bitterly that the long-awaited summers are marred by mosquito attacks. Mosquitos and black flies were a persistant menace to the people who previously lived out on the Delta.

Longtime residents remember the "good old days" and dismiss today's complaints as nonsense.

"I was a reindeer herder in the bush with all that muskeg surrounding us. All the time the mosquitos would be covering you. I could scoop my hand and they would fill it. I used to put a handkerchief over my face and I'd have trouble breathing. The bugs would be just clouds around your head."
—Jimmy Gordon

"When Inuvik first started and they were just clearing the brush there was lots of bugs around. People would take some willow branches and walk along brushing the bugs away. It looked funny to see people 'swat' themselves. But not now. People today complain about the bugs but there aren't any compared to the old days."
—Catherine Mitchell

To combat bugs on the Delta, people built "smudges" – fires covered with grass to create smoke and fend off the pests.

As the Town of Inuvik developed, draining puddles and clearing surrounding bush gradually reduced the droves of mosquitos. The problem is minor now in comparison to the early days.

Today, residents poke fun at themselves and their environment by participating in an annual contest sponsored by the Inuvik Drum. They compete against each other to win the "First Mosquito Of The Year" contest. The rules are simple. They merely have to be the first person to appear at the Drum office with the fresh "evidence" in their hands.

An "Inukshuk" on the Dempster Highway south of Inuvik

LOOKING FORWARD
'Visions of the Future'

Any new development idea seems to attract skeptics only too willing to predict failure. Twenty-five years ago there were many people who believed that in spite of careful planning, Inuvik would never prosper. Time has proven them wrong.

After 25 years of growth and development Inuvik is on the brink of fulfilling the promise of its planning.

The next decade will be a time of change and growth. Native land claims will be settled, and will give Inuvik stability of growth. Devolution of government programs and institutions to the regions will bring to Inuvik facilities which are now located either in Yellowknife or southern Canada.

Major petroleum interests have made commitments to Canada's federal government in excess of 2.1 billion dollars to be spent over the next five years in development of the Beaufort and Delta regions.

Al Pluim, President of the Inuvik Chamber of Commerce puts it very simply: "Whether we are ready or not, the development will take place."

Inuvik will benefit from agreements which have been entered into by the government of Canada with development companies. It will stand as a service centre for the Western Arctic and the Alaskan north slope.

There is an air of expectation in the town these days – an eager looking forward to the future.

Economic prospects are bright. Ideas are being passed around in boardrooms, suggestions are put forth by committees. There is interest in the community as a whole about improving its economic base, and the firm desire to achieve stability.

Inuvik has a unique infrastructure, designed to expand under future industrial impact. It has an all-weather paved airport able to accommodate the large support aircraft required by industry. There is an existing river transportation system. There is an all-weather road linking Inuvik to the south year round, with the exception of one and a half to two months when freeze-up or break-up prevent road use. There are strong indications that a pipeline will be built in the next few years, and Inuvik, as the Delta's hub, would become a resource distribution centre.

Inuvik is today an administrative hub for two levels of government, territorial and federal. It is the education centre for the Delta it serves. It is a transportation centre for river traffic, road transport and airline supply. It has a wealth of established private industry and is a commercial, educational and industrial distribution centre in every sense of the word. It has more than fulfilled the dreams of those whose vision looked to the North: it has surpassed those dreams.

It has, and will continue to have, a balance between industry, government and private activities to keep the economy reasonably stable.

A majority of the businesses now operating in Inuvik were established during the rapid growth period of the 1960s and early 1970s. They have grown within the framework of the community, but have remained flexible enough to accommodate future development. Inuvik business people have established themselves as long-range planners, as people with the foresight required for Inuvik to assume a progressive position in harmony with proposed development.

But Canada's industry has sometimes suffered losses from lack of government and public support at crucial times, and the Inuvik area is no exception. The business sector of Inuvik is strongly pressing for the encouragement and support of new industry for the area.

"What we as business people have to remember is that we have to make industry aware of our aspirations and be aware of their problems. We have to give something in order to receive something. The end result will be gain for all, regardless of race, colour or creed."

—Al Pluim

Today the Delta stands on the brink of becoming an oil and gas region comparable in importance to Alberta. There is an abundance of both renewable and non-renewable resources in the Inuvik region which, combined, may possibly make it one of the great commercial centres of Canada.

INGAMO HALL

People in Inuvik have been dancing in Ingamo Hall since 1965. Back then it was only the old Hudson's Bay warehouse, a multi-coloured plywood structure.

The name "Ingamo" is actually a misspelling of the word "Indemo" a word coined from the Indian-Eskimo Association – a group responsible for initiating the idea of the Hall.

In 1974 when the old Hall needed replacing the idea of a log structure emerged. Over one thousand logs were floated down the Mackenzie River from Fort Simpson and Allan Crich, an experienced log worker from British Columbia, worked each log into place.

Bingos and bake sales were held to raise money. The Department of Indian and Northern Affairs provided $200,000 to offset the total cost of half a million dollars.

The 7,904 square foot structure was completed in 1979.

Today the Hall is used for craft sales, workshops, meetings, feasts, drum dancing, art shows and wedding receptions.

Inuvik, by virtue of being one of the few areas in the Western Arctic which has an abundant supply of crushed rock, level air strip, and an infrastructure the same as that of most modern Canadian towns, will grow at a steady pace, as Inuvik was originally intended to do, to fulfill the educational and administrative needs of the people of the Western Arctic.

The natural gas pipeline which could also serve the community will be a reality within the next few years. With a source of relatively inexpensive energy, Inuvik could expand into the processing and secondary manufacturing areas.

Natural gas and spinoffs from hydrocarbon development around Inuvik, will help reduce the high cost of fuel oil and oil-based electricity.

In 1979 the Dempster Highway opened a new era of the travel industry. Curious tourists "invaded" the Arctic. As a transportation hub and a very important tourist centre, Inuvik can look forward to increasing improvements to the Dempster Highway in the form of widening and paving programs.

But Inuvik's most important resource has always been and will continue to be, its people.

The pioneer spirit is as unique a part of Inuvik as its far Northern location.

Inuvik has always been characterized by the ability of its people to pick up and carry on, to weather the ups and downs of a fluctuating economy. They are resilient, hardy Northern people. What incentives will encourage people to stay in the North? The answer lies in continued public policies which prompt people to come to the North from southern Canada; and ensure the continued presence of native people in the region.

"The tenacity and perseverance of the people who call Inuvik their home have pulled them through the tough times and stand them in good stead for the future."

—*Dave Nickerson, M.P.*

The long, cold, dark winters of Canada's Arctic have inspired imaginative ideas about making the environment more palatable. Suggestion has been made to build a large polythene dome that would completely cover the town and lessen the bitter effects of winter.

It is doubtful, however, whether the stubborn individualism of the people of Inuvik would ever welcome such an attempt to control their lives.

Only 30 years ago the land on which Inuvik is built was a hunter's trapline.

Today large commercial jets arrive from southern Canada carrying a precious cargo of foreign diplomats and prime ministers. On any given evening in a bar in Inuvik you could share a table with a cabinet minister, an IBM executive or the president of an oil company.

Canada's northern "model" town. A town that has turned the eyes of southern Canadians northward. A town whose people have endured a lifetime of joking comments about its "perfection". A town where people maintain their sense of humour in personal defence of their environment.

"Some people say Inuvik will be a nice place when it's finished. I happen to think it's not a bad place as it is."

—*Jim Robertson*

There is a romance about Canada's North. Folklore says that once smitten you become part of it. No matter how many miles or years you put between yourself and the North — you can never really leave.

You cannot pass through the North without being filled with memories of the people, the places, the breathtaking grandeur of the country. Most people keep their memories locked away. Bob Ruzicka was one man who came to the North. When he left, he put his memories to lyrics for all of us to share.

"I Remember"

I went down to the airport
I had time on my hands
And I watched the northern mainliner
Coming in to land

And I watched the people getting off that thing
And half a million memories flashed through my brain

I remember watching sunrise and the sun set over lunch
I remember the sound of mukluks on the boardwalk going crunch
I remember how the midnight sun would keep me awake
I remember walks in springtime up the hill to Hidden Lake
I remember it well...

I remember the smell of moosehide and the smell of burning wood
I remember Freddie Carmichael a local boy made good
I remember Agnes Semmler with her warm and laughing face
I remember going to the Zoo – yeah that's the wildest place
I remember it well...

I remember Delta Roundup
I remember Paulatuk
I remember eating oranges that cost a half a buck

I remember going up to Sachs and buying seal skins
And Father Adam in the morning praying for my sins
I remember it well...

I remember howling sled dogs that sent shivers up my spine
And parties at the Legion where we sure did have a good time
I remember people waiting for the barges to come in
And wishing that the ice cream didn't always taste like klim
I remember it well...
Yes...I remember

The softball and the curling games that never seem to end
The black flies and mosquitos that could drive you round the bend
Those winds in Tuktoyaktuk where you couldn't see or breathe
The stories 'bout the bushmen that the old folks still believe
I remember it well...

I remember Mother Hubbards – all the Hondas and Skidoos
The white kids in their moccasins, the native kids in shoes
I remember eating caribou in the darkness after day
And wondering how the natives knew Aklavik wouldn't wash away
I remember it well...

Now I'm down here in the city the weather's fine the grass is green
It's colder friends in some ways than the north has ever been
I love your life
I love your land
And I will not forget
Those places that I've travelled to
Those people that I've met

I remember them well...
Yes...I remember...

Lyrics by Bob Ruzicka
Printed With Permission
©1975 Copyright
Pet-Mac Publishing
A Division of
Damon Productions Ltd.,
Edmonton, Alberta, Canada